MW00513271

Healthy Bread Machine Recipes

Don't Give Up the Pleasure of Bread Even if You Are on a Diet.
Carry on Your Diet Effortlessly With the Right Recipe for You
Among Gluten-Free, Vegetables, Low Carb and Guarantee
Yourself a Healthy Long Life

Denise Baker

Table of Contents

Introduction

Bread making machine, otherwise known as a bread maker, is a home-based appliance that transforms uncooked ingredients into bread. It is made up of a saucepan for bread (or "tin"), with one or more built-in paddles at the bottom, present in the center of a small special-purpose oven. This little oven is usually operated via a control panel via a simple in-built computer utilizing the input settings. Some bread machines have diverse cycles for various forms of dough — together with white bread, whole grain, European-style (occasionally called "French"), and dough-only (for pizza dough and formed loaves baked in a traditional oven). Many also have a timer to enable the bread machine to work without the operator's attendance, and some high-end models allow the user to prog a customized period.

Bread makers are also fitted with a timer for testing when bread-making starts. For example, this allows them to be loaded at night but only begin baking in the morning to produce freshly baked bread for breakfast. They may also be set only for making dough, for example, for making pizza. Apart from bread, some can also be set to make other things like jam, pasta dough, and Japanese rice cake. Some of the new developments in the facility of the machine includes automatically adding nut. It also contains fruit from a tray during the kneading process. Bread makers typically take between three and four hours to bake a loaf. However, recent "quick bake" modes have become standard additions, many of which can produce a loaf in less than an hour.

When the bread has been baked, the bread maker removes the pan. Then leaving a slight indentation from the rod to which the paddle is connected. The finished loaf's shape is often regarded as unique. Many initial bread machines manufacture a vertically slanted towards, square, or cylindrical loaf that is significantly dissimilar from commercial bread; however, more recent units typically have a more conventional horizontal pan. Some bread machines use two paddles to form two lb. loaf in regular rectangle shape.

It takes the machine several hours to make a bread loaf. The products are rested first and brought to an optimal temperature. Stir with a paddle, and the ingredients are then shaped into flour. Use optimal temperature regulation, and the dough is then confirmed and then cooked.

To bake bread, ingredients are measured in a specified order into the bread pan (usually first liquids, with solid ingredients layered on top), and then the pan is put in the bread maker. The order of ingredients is important because contact with water triggers the instant yeast used in bread makers, so the yeast and water have to be kept separate until the prog starts.

Bread machine recipes are often much smaller than regular bread recipes. Sometimes standardized based on the machine's pan capacity, the most popular in the US market is 1.5lb./700 g units. Most recipes are written for that capacity; however, two lb. /900 g units are not uncommon. There are prepared bread mixes, specially made for bread makers, containing pre-measured ingredients and flour and yeast, flavorings, and sometimes dough conditioners.

Gluten-Free Bread Recipes

1. *Gluten-Free Simple Sandwich Bread*

Preparation Time: 5 Minutes

Cooking Time: 60 Minutes

Servings: 12

Ingredients:

- 1 1/2 cups sorghum flour

- 1 cup tapioca starch or potato starch

- 1/3 cup gluten-free millet flour or gluten-free oat flour

- 2 teaspoons xanthan gum

- 1 1/4 teaspoons fine sea salt

- 2 1/2 teaspoons gluten-free yeast for bread machines

- 1 1/4 cups warm water

- 3 tablespoons extra virgin olive oil

- 1 tablespoon honey or raw agave nectar

- 1/2 teaspoon mild rice vinegar or lemon juice

- 2 organic free-range eggs, beaten

Directions:

1. Blend the dry ingredients except for the yeast and set aside.

2. Add the liquid ingredients to the bread maker pan first, then gently pour the mixed dry ingredients on top of the liquid.

3. Make a well in the center part of the dry ingredients and add the yeast.

4. Set for Rapid 1 hour 20 minutes, medium crust color, and press Start.

5. In the end, put it on a cooling rack for 15 minutes before slicing to serve.

Nutrition:
- Calories: 137
- Sodium: 85 mg
- Dietary Fiber: 2.7 g
- Fat: 4.6 g
- Carbs: 22.1 g
- Protein: 2.4 g

2. *Gluten-Free Sourdough Bread*

Preparation Time: 5 Minutes

Cooking Time: 3 Hours

Servings: 12

Ingredients:

- 1 cup of water

- 3 eggs

- 3/4 cup ricotta cheese

- 1/4 cup honey

- 1/4 cup vegetable oil

- 1 teaspoon cider vinegar

- 3/4 cup gluten-free sourdough starter

- 2 cups white rice flour

- 2/3 cup potato starch

- 1/3 cup tapioca flour

- 1/2 cup dry milk powder

- 3 1/2 teaspoons xanthan gum

- 1 1/2 teaspoons salt

Directions:

1. Combine wet ingredients and pour into bread maker pan.

2. Mix dry ingredients in a large mixing bowl, and add on top of the wet ingredients.

3. Select the Gluten-Free cycle and press Start.

4. Remove the pan from the machine and allow the bread to remain in the pan for approximately 10 minutes.

5. Transfer to a cooling rack before slicing.

Nutrition:

- Calories: 299
- Sodium: 327 mg
- Dietary Fiber: 1.0 g
- Fat: 7.3 g
- Carbs: 46 g
- Protein: 5.2 g

3. *Gluten-Free Crusty Boule Bread*

Preparation Time: 15 Minutes

Cooking Time: 3 Hours

Servings: 12

Ingredients:

- 3 1/4 cups gluten-free flour mix

- 1 tablespoon active dry yeast

- 1 1/2 teaspoons kosher salt

- 1 tablespoon guar gum

- 1 1/3 cups warm water

- 2 large eggs, room temperature

- 2 tablespoons, plus two teaspoons olive oil

- 1 tablespoon honey

Directions:

1. Combine all of the dry ingredients, do not include the yeast, in a large mixing bowl; set aside.

2. Mix the water, eggs, oil, and honey in a separate mixing bowl.

3. Pour the wet ingredients into the bread maker.

4. I am adding the dry ingredients on top of the wet ingredients.

5. Form a well in the center part of the dry ingredients and add the yeast.

6. Set to Gluten-Free setting and press Start.

7. Remove baked bread and allow it to cool completely. Hollow out and fill with soup or dip to use as a boule or slice for serving.

Nutrition:
- Calories: 480
- Sodium: 490 mg
- Dietary Fiber: 67.9 g
- Fat: 3.2 g
- Carbs: 103.9 g
- Protein: 2.4 g

4. *Gluten-Free Brown Bread*

Preparation Time: 5 Minutes

Cooking Time: 3 Hours

Servings: 12

Ingredients:

- 2 large eggs, lightly beaten

- 1 3/4 cups warm water

- 3 tablespoons canola oil

- 1 cup brown rice flour

- 3/4 cup oat flour

- 1/4 cup tapioca starch

- 1 1/4 cups potato starch

- 1 1/2 teaspoons salt

- 2 tablespoons brown sugar

- 2 tablespoons gluten-free flaxseed meal

- 1/2 cup nonfat dry milk powder

- 2 1/2 teaspoons xanthan gum

- 3 tablespoons psyllium, whole husks

- 2 1/2 teaspoons gluten-free yeast for bread machines

Directions:

1. Add the eggs, water, and canola oil to the bread maker pan and stir until combined.

2. Whisk all of the dry ingredients except the yeast together in a large mixing bowl.

3. Add the dry ingredients on topmost of the wet ingredients.

4. Create a well in the center of the dry ingredients and add the yeast.

5. Set Gluten-Free cycle, medium crust color, and then press Start.

6. When the bread is done, lay the pan on its side to cool before slicing to serve.

Nutrition:

- Calories: 201
- Sodium: 390 mg
- Dietary Fiber: 10.6 g
- Fat: 5.7 g
- Carbs: 35.5 g
- Protein: 5.1 g

5. *Gluten-Free Potato Bread*

Preparation Time: 5 Minutes

Cooking Time: 3 Hours

Servings: 12

Ingredients:

- 1 medium russet potato, baked, or mashed leftovers

- 2 packets gluten-free quick yeast

- 3 tablespoons honey

- 3/4 cup warm almond milk

- 2 eggs, one egg white

- 3 2/3 cups almond flour

- 3/4 cup tapioca flour

- 1 teaspoon sea salt

- 1 teaspoon dried chive

- 1 tablespoon apple cider vinegar

- 1/4 cup olive oil

Directions:

1. Combine the entire dry ingredients, except the yeast, in a large mixing bowl; set aside.

2. Whisk together the milk, eggs, oil, apple cider, and honey in a separate mixing bowl.

3. Pour the wet ingredients into the bread maker.

4. Add the dry ingredients on top of the wet ingredients.

5. Produce a well in the dry ingredients and add the yeast.

6. Set to Gluten-Free bread setting, light crust color, and press Start.

7. Allow cooling completely before slicing.

Nutrition:

- Calories: 232
- Sodium: 173 mg
- Dietary Fiber: 6.3 g
- Fat: 13.2 g
- Carbs: 17.4 g
- Protein: 10.4 g

6. *Easy Gluten-Free, Dairy-Free Bread*

Preparation Time: 15 Minutes

Cooking Time: 2 Hours and 10 Minutes

Servings: 12

Ingredients:

- 1 1/2 cups warm water

- 2 teaspoons active dry yeast

- 2 teaspoons sugar

- 2 eggs, room temperature

- 1 egg white, room temperature

- 1 1/2 tablespoons apple cider vinegar

- 4 1/2 tablespoons olive oil

- 3 1/3 cups multi-purpose gluten-free flour

Directions:

1. Start with adding the yeast and sugar to the water, then stir to mix in a large mixing bowl; set aside until foamy, about 8 to 10 minutes.

2. Whisk the two eggs and one egg white together in a separate mixing bowl and add to the bread maker's baking pan.

3. Pour apple cider vinegar and oil into the baking pan.

4. Add foamy yeast/water mixture to baking pan.

5. Add the multi-purpose gluten-free flour on top.

6. Set for Gluten-Free bread setting and Start.

7. Remove and invert the pan onto a cooling rack to remove the bread from the baking pan. Allow cooling completely before slicing to serve.

Nutrition:

- Calories: 241
- Sodium: 164 mg
- Dietary Fiber: 5.6 g
- Fat: 6.8 g
- Carbs: 41 g
- Protein: 4.5 g

7. *Grain-Free Chia Bread*

Preparation Time: 5 Minutes

Cooking Time: 3 Hours

Servings: 12

Ingredients:

- 1 cup of warm water

- 3 large organic eggs, room temperature

- 1/4 cup olive oil

- 1 tablespoon apple cider vinegar

- 1 cup gluten-free chia seeds, ground to flour

- 1 cup almond meal flour

- 1/2 cup potato starch

- 1/4 cup coconut flour

- 3/4 cup millet flour

- 1 tablespoon xanthan gum

- 1 1/2 teaspoons salt

- 2 tablespoons sugar

- 3 tablespoons nonfat dry milk

- 6 teaspoons instant yeast

Directions:

1. Whisk wet ingredients together and place them in the bread maker pan.

2. Whisk dry ingredients, except yeast, together, and add on top of wet ingredients.

3. Make a well in the dry ingredients and add yeast.

4. Select the Whole Wheat cycle, light crust color, and press Start.

5. Allow cooling completely before serving.

Nutrition:

- Calories: 375
- Sodium: 462 mg
- Dietary Fiber: 22.3 g
- Fat: 18.3 g
- Carbs: 42 g
- Protein: 12.2 g

8. *Sorghum Bread*

Preparation Time: 5 Minutes

Cooking Time: 3 Hours

Servings: 12

Ingredients:

- 1 1/2 cups sorghum flour

- 1/2 cup tapioca starch

- 1/2 cup brown rice flour

- 1 teaspoon xanthan gum

- 1 teaspoon guar gum

- 1/3 teaspoon salt

- 3 tablespoons sugar

- 2 1/4 teaspoons instant yeast

- 3 eggs (room temperature, lightly beaten)

- 1/4 cup oil

- 1 1/2 teaspoons vinegar

- 3/4-1 cup milk (105-115°F)

Directions:

1. Blend the dry ingredients in a bowl, not including the yeast.

2. Add the wet ingredients to the bread maker pan, then add the dry ingredients on top.

3. Next is making a well in the center of the dry ingredients and add the yeast.

4. Set to Basic bread cycle, light crust color, and press Start.

5. Remove and lay on its side to cool on a wire rack before serving.

Nutrition:

- Calories: 169
- Sodium: 151 mg
- Dietary Fiber: 2.5 g
- Fat: 6.3 g
- Carbs: 25.8 g
- Protein: 3.3 g

9. *Paleo Bread*

Preparation Time: 10 Minutes

Cooking Time: 3 Hours and 15 Minutes

Servings: 16

Ingredients:

- 4 tablespoons chia seeds

- 1 tablespoon flax meal

- 3/4 cup, plus one tablespoon water

- 1/4 cup coconut oil

- 3 eggs, room temperature

- 1/2 cup almond milk

- 1 tablespoon honey

- 2 cups almond flour

- 1 1/4 cups tapioca flour

- 1/3 cup coconut flour

- 1 teaspoon salt

- 1/4 cup flax meal

- 2 teaspoons cream of tartar

- 1 teaspoon baking soda

- 2 teaspoons active dry yeast

Directions:

1. Combine the chia seeds plus a tablespoon of flax meal in a mixing bowl; stir in the water, and set aside.

2. Dissolve the coconut oil in a dish, and let it cool down to lukewarm.

3. Whisk in the eggs, almond milk, and honey.

4. Whisk in the chia seeds and flax meal gel and pour it into the bread maker pan.

5. Stir the almond flour, tapioca flour, coconut flour, salt, and 1/4 cup of flax meal.

6. Whisk the cream of tartar and baking soda in a separate bowl and combine it with the other dry ingredients.

7. Put the dry ingredients into the bread machine.

8. Make a little well on top and add the yeast.

9. Start the machine on the Wheat cycle, light or medium crust color, and press Start.

10. Remove to cool completely before slicing to serve.

Nutrition:

- Calories: 190
- Sodium: 243 mg
- Dietary Fiber: 5.2 g
- Fat: 10.3 g
- Carbs: 20.4 g
- Protein: 4.5 g

10. *Gluten-Free Oat and Honey Bread*

Preparation Time: 5 Minutes

Cooking Time: 3 Hours

Servings: 12

Ingredients:

- 1 1/4 cups warm water

- 3 tablespoons honey

- 2 eggs

- 3 tablespoons butter, melted

- 1 1/4 cups gluten-free oats

- 1 1/4 cups brown rice flour

- 1/2 cup potato starch

- 2 teaspoons xanthan gum

- 1 1/2 teaspoons sugar

- 3/4 teaspoon salt

- 1 1/2 tablespoons active dry yeast

Directions:

1. Add ingredients in the order listed above, except for the yeast.

2. Then form a well in the center of the dry ingredients and add the yeast.

3. Select the Gluten-Free cycle, light crust color, and press Start.

4. Remove bread and allow the bread to cool on its side on a cooling rack for 20 minutes before slicing to serve.

Nutrition:

- Calories: 151
- Sodium: 265 mg
- Dietary Fiber: 4.3 g
- Fat: 4.5 g
- Carbs: 27.2 g
- Protein: 3.5 g

11. *Oat Sourdough Loaf*

Preparation Time: 10 Minutes

Cooking Time: 25 Minutes

Servings: 8

Ingredients:

- 3 cups whole wheat or bread flour

- 250 g starter (see Sourdough Starter recipe)

- 1/2 cup water

- 3 tbsp. honey

- 1 tbsp. dark brown sugar or honey

- 1 stick butter, melted

- 1 tbsp. instant yeast

- 1 tsp. salt

- 3/4 quick-cooking oatmeal

Directions:

1. Preparing the ingredients. Grind the oatmeal through the food processor. Next is merging it with the rest of the dry ingredients, except yeast, in a bowl.

2. Place all the liquid ingredients in the bread pan. Add the starter, dry mix, then the yeast.

3. Put the pan in the Cuisinart bread machine.

4. Select the Bake cycle. Choose Artisan Dough. Press start and stand by until the loaf is cooked.

5. The machine will start the keep warm mode after the bread is complete.

6. Allow it to remain in that mode for about 10 minutes before unplugging.

7. Remove the pan and let it cool down for about 10 minutes.

Nutrition:

- Calories: 151
- Sodium: 265 mg
- Dietary Fiber: 4.3 g
- Fat: 4.5 g
- Carbs: 27.2 g
- Protein: 3.5 g

12. *Vegan Gluten-Free Bread*

Preparation Time: 10 Minutes

Cooking Time: 25 Minutes

Servings: 8

Ingredients:

- 1 cup almond flour

- 1 cup brown or white rice flour

- 2 tbsp. potato flour

- 4 tsp. baking powder

- 1/4 tsp. baking soda

- 1 cup almond milk

- 1 tbsp. white vinegar

Directions:

1. Place all ingredients in the Cuisinart bread pan in the liquid-dry-yeast layering.

2. Put the pan in the Cuisinart bread machine.

3. Select the Bake cycle. Choose Gluten Free.

4. Press start and wait until the loaf is cooked.

5. The machine will start the keep warm mode after the bread is complete.

6. Let it stay in that mode for at least 10 minutes before unplugging.

7. Remove the pan and let it cool down for about 10 minutes.

Nutrition:

- Calories: 151
- Sodium: 265 mg
- Dietary Fiber: 4.3 g
- Fat: 4.5 g
- Carbs: 27.2 g
- Protein: 3.5 g

13. *Gluten-Free Hawaiian Loaf*

Preparation Time: 10 Minutes

Cooking Time: 25 Minutes

Servings: 8

Ingredients:

- 4 cups gluten-free four

- 1 tsp. xanthan gum

- 2 1/2 tsp. (bread yeast should be gluten-free, but always check)

- 1/4 cup white sugar

- 1/2 cup softened butter

- 1 egg, beaten

- 1 cup fresh pineapple juice, warm

- 1/2 tsp. salt

- 1 tsp. vanilla extract

Directions:

1. Place all ingredients in the Cuisinart bread pan in the liquid-dry-yeast layering.

2. Put the pan in the Cuisinart bread machine.

3. Select the Bake cycle. Choose Gluten Free. Press open and wait until the loaf is cooked.

4. The machine will start the keep warm mode after the bread is complete.

5. Let it stay in that mode for 10 minutes before unplugging.

6. Remove the pan and let it cool down for about 10 minutes.

Nutrition:

- Calories: 151
- Sodium: 265 mg
- Dietary Fiber: 4.3 g
- Fat: 4.5 g
- Carbs: 27.2 g
- Protein: 3.5 g

14. *Multigrain Sourdough Loaf*

Preparation Time: 10 Minutes

Cooking Time: 25 Minutes

Servings: 8

Ingredients:

- 2/3 cup water, at 80°F to 90°F

- ¾ cup Simple Sourdough Starter (See Sourdough Starter recipe), fed, active, and at room temperature

- 2 tablespoons melted butter, cooled

- 2½ tablespoons sugar

- ¾ teaspoon salt

- ¾ cup multigrain cereal (Bob's Red Mill or equivalent)

- 2 2/3 cups white bread flour

- 1½ teaspoons bread machine or instant yeast

Directions:

1. Preparing the ingredients. Place the ingredients in your Cuisinart bread machine.

2. Select the Bake cycle. Prog the machine for Whole-Grain bread, select light or medium crust, and press Start.

3. When the loaf is finished, remove the bucket from the machine.

4. Let the loaf cool for 5 minutes.

5. Gently shake the bucket to get the loaf.

6. Turn it out onto a cooling rack.

Nutrition:

- Calories: 151
- Sodium: 265 mg
- Dietary Fiber: 4.3 g
- Fat: 4.5 g
- Carbs: 27.2 g
- Protein: 3.5 g

15. *Brown Rice Bread*

Preparation Time: 10 Minutes

Cooking Time: 25 Minutes

Servings: 8

Ingredients:

- Brown rice flour

- 2 eggs

- 1 1/4 cup almond milk

- 1 tsp. vinegar

- 1/2 cup coconut oil

- 2 tbsp. sugar

- 1/2 tsp. salt

- 2 1/4 tsp. instant yeast

Directions:

1. Place all ingredients in the Cuisinart bread pan in the liquid-dry-yeast layering.

2. Put the pan in the Cuisinart bread machine.

3. Select the Bake cycle. Choose Gluten-free. Press Start.

4. 5 minutes into the kneading process, pause the machine and check the consistency of the dough. Add more flour if necessary.

5. Resume and wait until the loaf is cooked.

6. The machine will start the keep warm mode after the bread is complete.

7. Make it stay in that mode for about 10 minutes before unplugging.

8. Remove the pan and let it cool down for about 10 minutes.

Nutrition:

- Calories: 151
- Sodium: 265 mg
- Dietary Fiber: 4.3 g
- Fat: 4.5 g
- Carbs: 27.2 g
- Protein: 3.5 g

16. *Gluten-Free White Bread*

Preparation Time: 10 Minutes

Cooking Time: 25 Minutes

Servings: 8

Ingredients:

- 2 cups white rice flour

- 1 cup potato starch

- 1/2 cup soy flour

- 1/2 cup cornstarch

44

- 1 tsp. vinegar

- 1 tsp. xanthan gum

- 1 tsp. instant yeast (bread yeast should be gluten-free, but always check)

- 1 1/4 cup buttermilk

- 3 eggs

- 1/4 cup sugar or honey

- 1/4 cup coconut or olive oil

Directions:

1. Place all ingredients in the Cuisinart bread pan in the liquid-dry-yeast layering.

2. Put the pan in the Cuisinart bread machine.

3. Select the Bake cycle. Choose Gluten Free. Press Start.

4. 5 minutes into the kneading process, pause the machine and check the firmness of the dough. Add more flour if necessary.

5. Resume and wait until the loaf is cooked.

6. The machine will start the keep warm mode after the bread is complete.

7. Allow it to stay in that mode for about 10 minutes before unplugging.

8. Remove the pan and let it cool down for about 10 minutes.

Nutrition:

- Calories: 151
- Sodium: 265 mg
- Dietary Fiber: 4.3 g
- Fat: 4.5 g
- Carbs: 27.2 g
- Protein: 3.5 g

Low-Carb Bread Recipes

17. *Pumpkin Bread*

Preparation Time: 5 minutes

Cooking Time: 1 hour

Servings: 14

Ingredients:

- ½ cup plus 2 tablespoons warm water

- ½ cup canned pumpkin puree

- ¼ cup butter, softened

- ¼ cup non-fat dry milk powder

- 2¾ cups bread flour

- ¼ cup brown sugar

- ¾ teaspoon salt

- 1 teaspoon ground cinnamon

- ½ teaspoon ground ginger

- 1/8 teaspoon ground nutmeg

- 2¼ teaspoons active dry yeast

Directions:

1. Place all ingredients in the baking pan of the bread machine in the order recommended by the manufacturer.

2. Place the baking pan in the bread machine and close the lid.

3. Select Basic setting.

4. Press the start button.

5. Carefully, remove the baking pan from the machine and then invert the bread loaf onto a wire rack to cool completely before slicing.

6. With a sharp knife, cut bread loaf into desired-sized slices and serve.

Nutrition:

- Calories 134
- Total Fat 3.6 g
- Saturated Fat 2.1 g
- Cholesterol 9 mg
- Sodium 149 mg
- Total Carbs 22.4 g
- Fiber 1.1 g
- Sugar 2.9 g
- Protein 2.9 g

18. *Cranberry Bread*

Preparation Time: 10 minutes

Cooking Time: 3 hours

Servings: 16

Ingredients:

- 1 cup plus 3 tablespoons water

- ¼ cup honey

- 2 tablespoons butter, softened

- 5 cups bread flour

- 1 teaspoon salt

- 2 teaspoons bread machine yeast

- ¾ cup dried cranberries

Directions:

1. Place all ingredients (except the cranberries) in the baking pan of the bread machine in the order recommended by the manufacturer.

2. Place the baking pan in the bread machine and close the lid.

3. Select sweet bread setting.

4. Press the start button.

5. Wait for the bread machine to beep before adding the cranberries.

6. Carefully, remove the baking pan from the machine and then invert the bread loaf onto a wire rack to cool completely before slicing.

7. With a sharp knife, cut bread loaf into desired-sized slices and serve.

Nutrition:

- Calories 147
- Total Fat 1.8 g
- Saturated Fat 1 g
- Cholesterol 4 mg
- Sodium 159 mg
- Total Carbs 28.97 g
- Fiber 1.2 g
- Sugar 4.6 g
- Protein 3.5 g

19. *Cranberry Orange Bread*

Preparation Time: 10 minutes

Cooking Time: 3 hours

Servings: 12

Ingredients:

- 3 cups all-purpose flour

- 1 cup dried cranberries

- ¾ cup plain yogurt

- ½ cup warm water

- 3 tablespoons honey

- 1 tablespoon butter, melted

- 2 teaspoons active dry yeast

- 1½ teaspoons salt

- 1 teaspoon orange oil

Directions:

1. Place all ingredients in the baking pan of the bread machine in the order recommended by the manufacturer.

2. Place the baking pan in the bread machine and close the lid.

3. Select Basic setting and then Light Crust.

4. Press the start button.

5. Carefully, remove the baking pan from the machine and then invert the bread loaf onto a wire rack to cool completely before slicing.

6. With a sharp knife, cut bread loaf into desired-sized slices and serve.

Nutrition:

- Calories 166
- Total Fat 2.7 g
- Saturated Fat 1 g
- Cholesterol 3 mg
- Sodium 309 mg
- Total Carbs 30.4 g
- Fiber 1.3 g
- Sugar 5.8 g
- Protein 4.4 g

20. *Orange Bread*

Preparation Time: 10 minutes

Cooking Time: 3 hours

Servings: 12

Ingredients:

- 1¼ cups water

- 3 tablespoons powdered milk

- 1½ tablespoons vegetable oil

- 3 tablespoons honey

- 2½ cups bread flour

- ¾ cup amaranth flour

- 1/3 cup whole-wheat flour

- ¾ teaspoon salt

- 3 tablespoons fresh orange zest, grated finely

- 2¼ teaspoons active dry yeast

Directions:

1. Place all ingredients in the baking pan of the bread machine in the order recommended by the manufacturer.

2. Place the baking pan in the bread machine and close the lid.

3. Select Basic setting.

4. Press the start button.

5. Carefully, remove the baking pan from the machine and then invert the bread loaf onto a wire rack to cool completely before slicing.

6. With a sharp knife, cut bread loaf into desired-sized slices and serve.

Nutrition:

- Calories 197
- Total Fat 2.9 g
- Saturated Fat 0.6 g
- Cholesterol 0 mg
- Sodium 162 mg
- Total Carbs 36.9 g
- Fiber 2.6 g
- Sugar 5.6 g
- Protein 6.1 g

21. *Pumpkin Cranberry Bread*

Preparation Time: 10 minutes

Cooking Time: 4 hours

Servings: 12

Ingredients:

- ¾ cup water

- 2/3 cup canned pumpkin

- 3 tablespoons brown sugar

- 2 tablespoons vegetable oil

- 2 cups all-purpose flour

- 1 cup whole-wheat flour

- 1¼ teaspoon salt

- ½ cup sweetened dried cranberries

- ½ cup walnuts, chopped

- 1¾ teaspoons active dry yeast

Directions:

1. Place all ingredients in the baking pan of the bread machine in the order recommended by the manufacturer.

2. Place the baking pan in the bread machine and close the lid.

3. Select Basic setting.

4. Press the start button.

5. Carefully, remove the baking pan from the machine and then invert the bread loaf onto a wire rack to cool completely before slicing.

6. With a sharp knife, cut bread loaf into desired-sized slices and serve.

Nutrition:

- Calories 199
- Total Fat 6 g
- Saturated Fat 0.7 g
- Cholesterol 0 mg
- Sodium 247 mg
- Total Carbs 31.4 g
- Fiber 3.2 g
- Sugar 5.1 g
- Protein 5.6 g

22. *Banana Chocolate Chip Bread*

Preparation Time: 10 minutes

Cooking Time: 1 hour 40 minutes

Servings: 16

Ingredients:

- ½ cup warm milk

- 2 eggs

- ½ cup butter, melted

- 1 teaspoon vanilla extract

- 3 medium ripe bananas, peeled and mashed

- 1 cup granulated white sugar

- 2 cups all-purpose flour

- ½ teaspoon salt

- 2 teaspoons baking powder

- 1 teaspoon baking soda

- ½ cup chocolate chips

Directions:

1. Add ingredients (except for cranberries) in the baking pan of the bread machine in the order recommended by the manufacturer.

2. Place the baking pan in the bread machine and close the lid.

3. Select Quick Bread setting.

4. Press the start button.

5. Wait for the bread machine to beep before adding the chocolate chips.

6. Carefully, remove the baking pan from the machine and then invert the bread loaf onto a wire rack to cool completely before slicing.

7. With a sharp knife, cut bread loaf into desired-sized slices and serve.

Nutrition:

- Calories 215
- Total Fat 8.2 g
- Saturated Fat 5 g
- Cholesterol 38 mg
- Sodium 210 mg
- Total Carbs 33.4 g
- Fiber 1.2 g
- Sugar 18.4 g
- Protein 3.2 g

23. *Gingerbread*

Preparation Time: 10 minutes

Cooking Time: 3 hours

Servings: 12

Ingredients:

- 3/4 cup milk

- 1/4 cup molasses

- 1 egg

- 3 tablespoons butter

- 3 1/3 cups bread flour

- 1 tablespoon brown sugar

- ¾ teaspoon salt

- ¾ teaspoon ground cinnamon

- ¾ teaspoon ground ginger

- 2¼ teaspoons active dry yeast

- 1/3 cup raisins

Directions:

1. Place all ingredients (except for raisins) in the baking pan of the bread machine in the order recommended by the manufacturer.

2. Place the baking pan in the bread machine and close the lid.

3. Select Basic setting and then Light Crust.

4. Press the start button.

5. Wait for the bread machine to beep before adding the raisins.

6. Carefully, remove the baking pan from the machine and then invert the bread loaf onto a wire rack to cool completely before slicing.

7. With a sharp knife, cut bread loaf into desired-sized slices and serve.

Nutrition:

- Calories 202
- Total Fat 4 g
- Saturated Fat 2.2 g
- Cholesterol 23 mg
- Sodium 184 mg
- Total Carbs 36.8 g
- Fiber 1.3 g
- Sugar 7.7 g
- Protein 5 g

24. *Raisin Cinnamon Swirl Bread*

Preparation Time: 15 minutes

Cooking Time: 3 hours 35 minutes

Servings: 12

Ingredients:

Dough:

- ¼ cup milk

- 1 large egg, beaten

- Water, as required

- ¼ cup butter, softened

- 1/3 cup white sugar

- 1 teaspoon salt

- 3½ cups bread flour

- 2 teaspoons active dry yeast

- ½ cup raisins

Cinnamon Swirl:

- 1/3 cup white sugar

- 3 teaspoons ground cinnamon

- 2 egg whites, beaten

- 1/3 cup butter, melted and cooled

Directions:

1. For bread: Place milk and egg into a small bowl.

2. Add enough water to make 1 cup of mixture.

3. Place the egg mixture into the baking pan of the bread machine.

4. Place the remaining ingredients (except for raisins) on top in the order recommended by the manufacturer.

5. Place the baking pan in the bread machine and close the lid.

6. Select Dough cycle.

7. Press the start button.

8. Wait for the bread machine to beep before adding the raisins.

9. After Dough cycle completes, remove the dough from the bread pan and place it onto a lightly floured surface.

10. Roll the dough into a 10x12-inch rectangle.

11. For the swirl: Mix together the sugar and cinnamon.

12. Brush the dough rectangle with 1 egg white, followed by the melted butter.

13. Now, sprinkle the dough with cinnamon sugar, leaving about a 1-inch border on each side.

14. From the short side, roll the dough and pinch the ends underneath.

15. Grease loaf pan and place the dough.

16. With a kitchen towel, cover the loaf pan and place in a warm place for 1 hour or until doubled in size.

17. Preheat your oven to 350°F.

18. Brush the top of the dough with the remaining egg white.

19. Bake for approximately 35 minutes or until a wooden skewer inserted in the center comes out clean.

20. Remove the bread pan and place it onto a wire rack to cool for about 15 minutes.

21. Cool bread before slicing

Nutrition:

- Calories 297
- Total Fat 10.6 g
- Saturated Fat 6.3 g
- Cholesterol 41 mg
- Sodium 277 mg
- Total Carbs 46.2 g
- Fiber 1.7 g
- Sugar 16.5 g
- Protein 5.6 g

Vegetable Bread

25. *Zero-Fat Carrot Pineapple Loaf*

Preparation Time: 20 minutes

Cooking Time: 1.5 hours

Serving Size: 1 ounce (28.3 g)

Ingredients:

- 2 ½ cups all-purpose flour

- ¾ cup of sugar

- ½ cup pineapples, crushed

- ½ cup carrots, grated

- ½ cup raisins

- 2 teaspoons baking powder

- ½ teaspoon ground cinnamon

- ½ teaspoon salt

- ¼ teaspoon allspice

- ¼ teaspoon nutmeg

- ½ cup applesauce

- 1 tablespoon molasses

Directions:

1. Put first the wet ingredients into the bread pan before the dry ingredients.

2. Press the "Quick" or "Cake" mode of your bread machine.

3. Allow the machine to complete all cycles.

4. Take out the pan from the machine, but wait for another 10 minutes before transferring the bread into a wire rack.

5. Cool down the bread before slicing.

Nutrition:

- Calories: 70
- Carbohydrates: 16 g
- Fat: 0 g
- Protein: 1 g

26. *Autumn Treasures Loaf*

Preparation Time: 15 minutes

Cooking Time: 1/5 hours

Serving Size: 1 ounce (28.3 g)

Ingredients:

- 1 cup all-purpose flour

- ½ cup dried fruit, chopped

- ¼ cup pecans, chopped

- ¼ cup of sugar

- 2 tablespoons baking powder

- 1 teaspoon salt

- ¼ teaspoon of baking soda

- ½ teaspoon ground nutmeg

- 1 cup apple juice

- ¼ cup of vegetable oil

- 3 tablespoons aquafaba

- 1 teaspoon of vanilla extract

Directions:

1. Add all wet ingredients first to the bread pan before the dry ingredients.

2. Turn on the bread machine with the "Quick" or "Cake" setting.

3. Wait for all cycles to be finished.

4. Remove the bread pan from the machine.

5. After 10 minutes, transfer the bread from the pan into a wire rack.

6. Slice the bread only when it has completely cooled down.

Nutrition:

- Calories: 80
- Carbohydrates: 12 g
- Fat: 3 g
- Protein: 1 g

27. *Oatmeal Walnut Bread*

Preparation Time: 15 minutes

Cooking Time: 1.5 hours

Serving Size: 1 ounce per serving

Ingredients:

- ¾ cup whole-wheat flour

- ¼ cup all-purpose flour

- ½ cup brown sugar

- 1/3 cup walnuts, chopped

- ¼ cup oatmeal

- ¼ teaspoon of baking soda

- 2 tablespoons baking powder

- 1 teaspoon salt

- 1 cup Vegan buttermilk

- ¼ cup of vegetable oil

- 3 tablespoons aquafaba

Directions:

1. Add into the bread pan the wet ingredients then followed by the dry ingredients.

2. Use the "Quick" or "Cake" setting of your bread machine.

3. Allow the cycles to be completed.

4. Take out the pan from the machine.

5. Wait for 10 minutes, then remove the bread from the pan.

6. Once the bread has cooled down, slice it and serve.

Nutrition:
- Calories: 80
- Carbohydrates: 11 g
- Fat: 3 g
- Protein: 2 g

28. *Banana-Lemon Loaf*

Preparation Time: 15 minutes

Cooking Time: 1.5 hours

Serving Size: 1 ounce (28.3 g)

Ingredients:

- 2 cups all-purpose flour

- 1 cup bananas, very ripe and mashed

- 1 cup walnuts, chopped

- 1 cup of sugar

- 1 tablespoon baking powder

- 1 teaspoon lemon peel, grated

- ½ teaspoon salt

- 2 eggs

- ½ cup of vegetable oil

- 2 tablespoons lemon juice

Directions:

1. Put all ingredients into a pan in this order: bananas, wet ingredients, and then dry ingredients.

2. Press the "Quick" or "Cake" setting of your bread machine.

3. Allow the cycles to be completed.

4. Take out the pan from the machine. Then cool down for 10 minutes before slicing the bread enjoy.

Nutrition:

- Calories: 120
- Carbohydrates: 15 g
- Fat: 6 g
- Protein: 2 g

29. *Black Forest Loaf*

Preparation Time: 20 minutes

Cooking Time: 3 hours

Serving Size: 2 ounces (56.7 g)

Ingredients:

- 1 ½ cups bread flour

- 1 cup whole wheat flour

- 1 cup rye flour

- 3 tablespoons cocoa

- 1 tablespoon caraway seeds

- 2 teaspoons yeast

- 1 ½ teaspoons salt

- 1 ¼ cups water

- 1/3 cup molasses

- 1 ½ tablespoon canola oil

Directions:

1. Combine the ingredients in the bread pan by putting the wet ingredients first, followed by the dry ones.

2. Press the "Normal" or "Basic" mode and light the bread machine's crust color setting.

3. After the cycles are completed, take out the bread from the machine.

4. Cool down and then slice the bread.

Nutrition:

- Calories: 136
- Carbohydrates: 27 g
- Fat: 2 g
- Protein: 3 g

30. *Pumpkin Raisin Bread*

Preparation Time: 15 minutes

Cooking Time: 1.5 hours

Serving Size: 1 ounce (28.3 g)

Ingredients:

- ½ cup all-purpose flour

- ½ cup whole-wheat flour

- ½ cup pumpkin, mashed

- ½ cup raisins

- ¼ cup brown sugar

- 2 tablespoons baking powder

- 1 teaspoon salt

- 1 teaspoon pumpkin pie spice

- ¼ teaspoon baking soda

- ¾ cup apple juice

- ¼ cup of vegetable oil

- 3 tablespoons aquafaba

Directions:

1. Place all ingredients in the bread pan in this order: apple juice, pumpkin, oil, aquafaba, flour, sugar, baking powder, baking soda, salt, pumpkin pie spice, and raisins.

2. Select the "Quick" or "Cake" mode of your bread machine.

3. Let the machine finish all cycles.

4. Remove the pan from the machine.

5. After 10 minutes, transfer the bread to a wire rack.

6. Slice the bread only when it has completely cooled down.

Nutrition:

- Calories: 70
- Carbohydrates: 12 g
- Fat: 2 g
- Protein: 1 g

31. *Hawaiian Bread*

Preparation Time: 10 minutes

Cooking Time: 3 hours

Serving Size: 1 ounce (56.7 g)

Ingredients:

- 3 cups bread flour

- 2 ½ tablespoons brown sugar

- ¾ teaspoon salt

- 2 teaspoons quick-rising yeast

- 1 egg

- ¾ cup pineapple juice

- 2 tablespoons almond milk

- 2 tablespoons vegetable oil

Directions:

1. Pour all wet ingredients first into the bread pan before adding the dry ingredients.

2. Set the bread machine to "Basic" or "Normal" mode with a light crust color setting.

3. Allow the machine to finish the mixing, kneading, and baking cycles.

4. Take out the pan from the machine.

5. Transfer the bread to a wire rack.

6. After one hour, slice the bread and serve.

Nutrition:

- Calories: 169
- Carbohydrates: 30 g
- Fat: 3 g
- Protein: 4 g

32. *Sweet Potato Bread*

Preparation Time: 10 minutes

Cooking Time: 3 hours

Serving Size: 2 ounces (56.7 g)

Ingredients:

- 4 cups bread flour

- 1 cup sweet potatoes, mashed

- ½ cup brown sugar

- 2 teaspoons yeast

- 1 ½ teaspoon salt

- ½ teaspoon cinnamon

- ½ cup of water

- 2 tablespoons vegetable oil

- 1 teaspoon vanilla extract

Directions:

1. Add the wet ingredients first, then follow by dry ingredients to the bread pan.

2. Use the "Normal" or "Basic" mode of the bread machine.

3. Select the light or medium crust color setting.

4. Once the cycles are finished, take out the machine's bread, Cool down the bread on a wire rack before slicing and serving.

Nutrition:

- Calories: 111
- Carbohydrates: 21 g
- Fat: 2 g
- Protein: 3 g

33. *Orange Date Bread*

Preparation Time: 20 minutes

Cooking Time: 1.5 hours

Serving Size: 1 ounce (28.3 g)

Ingredients:

- 2 cups all-purpose flour

- 1 cup dates, chopped

- ¾ cup of sugar

- ½ cup walnuts, chopped

- 2 tablespoons orange rind, grated

- 1 ½ teaspoons baking powder

- 1 teaspoon baking soda

- ½ cup of orange juice

- ½ cup of water

- 1 tablespoon vegetable oil

- 1 teaspoon vanilla extract

Direction:

1. Put the wet ingredients then the dry ingredients into the bread pan.

2. Press the "Quick" or "Cake" mode of the bread machine.

3. Allow all cycles to be finished.

4. Remove the pan from the machine, but keep the bread in the pan for 10 minutes more.

5. Take out the bread from the pan, and let it cool down completely before slicing.

Nutrition:

- Calories: 80
- Carbohydrates: 14 g
- Fat: 2 g
- Protein: 1 g

34. *Vegan Cinnamon Raisin Bread*

Preparation Time: 10 minutes

Cooking Time: 3 hours

Serving Size: 2 ounces (56.7 g)

Ingredients:

- 2 ¼ cups oat flour

- ¾ cup raisins

- ½ cup almond flour

- ¼ cup of coconut sugar

- 2 ½ teaspoons cinnamon

- 1 teaspoon baking powder

- ½ teaspoon baking soda

- ¼ teaspoon salt

- ¾ cup of water

- ½ cup of soy milk

- ¼ cup maple syrup

- 3 tablespoons coconut oil

- 1 teaspoon vanilla extract

Directions:

1. Put all wet ingredients first into the bread pan, followed by the dry ingredients.

2. Set the bread machine to "Quick" or "Cake" mode.

3. Wait until the mixing and baking cycles are done.

4. Remove the pan from the machine.

5. Wait for another 10 minutes before transferring the bread to a wire rack.

6. After the bread has completely cooled down, slice it and serve.

Nutrition:

- Calories: 130
- Carbohydrates: 26 g
- Fat: 2 g
- Protein: 3 g

35. *Beer Bread*

Preparation Time: 10-15 minutes

Cooking Time: 2.5-3 hours

Serving Size: 2 ounces (56.7 g)

Ingredients:

- 3 cups bread flour

- 2 tablespoons sugar

- 2 ¼ teaspoons yeast

- 1 ½ teaspoons salt

- 2/3 cup beer

- 1/3 cup water

- 2 tablespoons vegetable oil

Direction:

1. Add all ingredients into a pan in this order: water, beer, oil, salt, sugar, flour, and yeast.

2. Start the bread machine with the "Basic" or "Normal" mode on and light to medium crust color.

3. Let the machine complete all cycles.

4. Take out the pan from the machine.

5. Transfer the beer bread into a wire rack to cool it down for about an hour.

6. Cut into 12 slices, and serve.

Nutrition:

- Calories: 130
- Carbohydrates: 25 g
- Fat: 1 g
- Protein: 4 g

36. *Onion and Mushroom Bread*

Preparation Time: 10 minutes

Cooking Time: 1 hour

Serving Size: 2 ounces (56.7 g)

Ingredients:

- 4 ounces mushrooms, chopped

- 4 cups bread flour

- 3 tablespoons sugar

- 4 teaspoons fast-acting yeast

- 4 teaspoons dried onions, minced

- 1 ½ teaspoons salt

- ½ teaspoon garlic powder

- ¾ cup of water

Directions:

1. Pour the water first into the bread pan, and then add all of the dry ingredients.

2. Press the "Fast" cycle mode of the bread machine.

3. Wait until all cycles are completed.

4. Transfer the bread from the pan into a wire rack.

5. Wait for one hour before slicing the bread into 12 pieces.

6. Serving Size: 2 ounces per slice

Nutrition:

- Calories: 120
- Carbohydrates: 25 g
- Fat: 0 g
- Protein: 5 g

37. *Healthy Celery Loaf*

Preparation Time: 2 hours 40 minutes

Cooking Time: 50 minutes

Servings: 1 loaf

Ingredients:

- 1 can (10 ounces) cream of celery soup

- 3 tablespoons low-fat milk, heated

- 1 tablespoon vegetable oil

- 1¼ teaspoons celery salt

- ¾ cup celery, fresh/sliced thin

- 1 tablespoon celery leaves, fresh, chopped

- 1 whole egg

- ¼ teaspoon sugar

- 3 cups bread flour

- ¼ teaspoon ginger

- ½ cup quick-cooking oats

- 2 tablespoons gluten

- 2 teaspoons celery seeds

- 1 pack of active dry yeast

Directions:

1. Add all of the ingredients into your bread machine, carefully following the instructions of the manufacturer

2. Set the prog of your bread machine to Basic/White Bread and set crust type to Medium

3. Press START

4. Wait until the cycle completes

5. Once the loaf is ready, take the bucket out and let the loaf cool for 5 minutes

6. Gently shake the bucket to remove the loaf

7. Transfer to a cooling rack, slice and serve

8. Enjoy!

Nutrition:

- Calories: 73
- Fat: 4 g
- Carbohydrates: 8 g
- Protein: 3 g
- Fiber: 1 g

38. *Zucchini Herbed Bread*

Preparation Time: 2 hours 20 minutes

Cooking Time: 50 minutes

Servings: 1 loaf

Ingredients:

- ½ cup water

- 1 teaspoon honey

- 1 tablespoons oil

- ¾ cup zucchini, grated

- ¾ cup whole wheat flour

- 3 cups bread flour

- 1 tablespoon fresh basil, chopped

- 1 teaspoon sesame seeds

- 1 teaspoon salt

- 1½ teaspoon active dry yeast

Directions:

1. Add all of the ingredients into your bread machine, carefully following the instructions of the manufacturer

2. Set the prog of your bread machine to Basic/White Bread and set crust type to Medium

3. Press START

4. Wait until the cycle completes

5. Once the loaf is ready, take the bucket out and let the loaf cool for 5 minutes

6. Gently shake the bucket to remove the loaf

7. Transfer to a cooling rack, slice and serve

8. Enjoy!

Nutrition:

- Calories: 153
- Fat: 1 g
- Carbohydrates: 28 g
- Protein: 5 g
- Fiber: 2 g

39. *Potato Bread*

Preparation Time: 3 hours

Cooking Time: 45 minutes

Servings: 2 loaves

Ingredients:

- 1 3/4 teaspoon active dry yeast

- 1 tablespoon dry milk

- 1/4 cup instant potato flakes

- 1 tablespoon sugar

- 6 cups bread flour

- 1 1/4 teaspoon salt

- 1 tablespoon butter

- 1 3/8 cups water

Directions:

1. Put all the liquid ingredients in the pan. Add all the dry ingredients, except the yeast. Form a shallow hole in the middle of the dry ingredients and place the yeast.

2. Secure the pan in the machine and close the lid. Choose the basic setting and your desired color of the crust. Press starts.

3. Allow the bread to cool before slicing.

Nutrition:

- Calories: 35
- Total Carbohydrate: 19 g
- Total Fat: 0 g
- Protein: 4 g

40.*Spinach Bread*

Preparation Time: 2 hours 20 minutes

Cooking Time: 40 minutes

Servings: 1 loaf

Ingredients:

- 1 cup water

- 1 tablespoon vegetable oil

- 1/2 cup frozen chopped spinach, thawed and drained

- 3 cups all-purpose flour

- 1/2 cup shredded Cheddar cheese

- 1 teaspoon salt

- 1 tablespoon white sugar

- 1/2 teaspoon ground black pepper

- 1/2 teaspoons active dry yeast

Directions:

1. In the pan of bread machine, put all ingredients according to the suggested order of manufacture. Set white bread cycle.

Nutrition:

- Calories: 121
- Total Carbohydrate: 20.5 g
- Cholesterol: 4 mg
- Total Fat: 2.5 g
- Protein: 4 g
- Sodium: 184 mg

41. *Potato Rosemary Bread*

Preparation Time: 3 hours

Cooking Time: 30 minutes

Servings: 20

Ingredients:

- 8 cups bread flour, sifted

- 1 tablespoon white sugar

- 1 tablespoon sunflower oil

- 1½ teaspoons salt

- 1½ cups lukewarm water

- 1 teaspoon active dry yeast

- 1 cup potatoes, mashed

- 3 teaspoons crushed rosemary

Directions:

1. Prepare all of the ingredients for your bread and measuring means (a cup, a spoon, kitchen scales).

2. Carefully measure the ingredients into the pan, except the potato and rosemary.

3. Place all of the ingredients into the bread bucket in the right order, following the manual for your bread machine.

4. Close the cover.

5. Select the prog of your bread machine to BREAD with FILLINGS and choose the crust color to MEDIUM.

6. Press START.

7. After the signal, put the mashed potato and rosemary into the dough.

8. Wait until the prog completes.

9. When done, take the bucket out and let it cool for 5-10 minutes.

10. Shake the loaf from the pan and let cool for 30 minutes on a cooling rack.

11. Slice, serve and enjoy the taste of fragrant homemade bread.

Nutrition:

- Calories: 106
- Total Carbohydrate: 21 g
- Total Fat: 1 g
- Protein: 2.9 g
- Sodium: 641 mg
- Fiber: 1 g
- Sugar: 0.8 g

Conclusion

This book has presented you to some of the easiest and delicious bread recipes you can find. 1 of the most mutual struggles for anyone following the diet is that they have to cut out so many of the foods they love, like sugary foods and starchy bread products. This book helps you overcome both those issues.

The bread machine comes with a set of instructions that you must learn from the manual to use it the right way. There is a certain way of loading the ingredients that must be followed, and the instructions vary according to the make and the model. So, when you first get a machine, sit down and learn the manual from start to finish; this allows you to put it to good use and get better results. The manual will tell you exactly what to put in it, as well as the correct settings to use, according to the different ingredients and the type of bread you want to make.

These loaves of bread are made using the normal ingredients you can find locally, so there's no need to have to order anything or have to go to any specialty stores for any of them. With these pieces of bread, you can enjoy the same meals you used to enjoy but stay on track with your diet as much as you want.

Focus your mindset toward the positive. Through a diet, you can help prevent diabetes, heart diseases, and respiratory problems. If you already feel pain from any of these, a diet under a doctor's supervision can greatly improve your condition.

Having a bread machine in your kitchen makes life easy. Whether you are a professional baker or a home cook, this appliance will help you get the best bread texture and flavors with minimum effort. Bread making is an art, and it takes extra care and special technique to deal with a specific type of flour and bread machine that enables you to do so even when you are not a professional. In this book, we have discussed all bread machines and how we can put them to good use. Basic information about flour and yeast is also discussed to give all the beginners an idea of how to deal with the major ingredients of bread and what variety to use to get a particular type of bread. And finally, some delicious bread recipes were shared so that you can try them at home!

Lose the weight you want to lose, feel great, and still get to indulge in that piping hot piece of bread now and then. Spread on your favorite topping, and your bread craving will be satisfied.

Moreover, we have learned that the bread machine is a vital tool to have in our kitchen. It is not that hard to put into use. All you need to learn is how it functions and what its features are. You also need to use it more often to learn the dos and don'ts of using the machine.